Original title:
Mystery's Mischief

Author: Juliana Wentworth
ISBN HARDBACK: 978-9916-90-310-0
ISBN PAPERBACK: 978-9916-90-311-7

Riddles in the iLuminated Fog

In the realm where shadows creep,
Secrets in the silence seep.
Soft whispers kiss the chilly air,
Found only in the fog's cold stare.

Mist wields its gentle charm,
Enfolding us in its soft arm.
Each step breathes a hidden tale,
Where light and dark gently veil.

Shapes emerge, then fade away,
Lost in hues of gray ballet.
Questions dance beneath the glow,
As riddles form in twirling flow.

Every heartbeat, every sigh,
Echoes of the night's reply.
In the fog's embrace we find,
Illusions cradled by the mind.

Whispers Through Time

In shadows cast by ancient trees,
Whispers float on a gentle breeze.
Echoes of laughter, tales of old,
Secrets wrapped in silence bold.

Moments linger, like fleeting dreams,
Threads of history in soft moonbeams.
Time dances on the edge of night,
Holding close what's lost from sight.

The Silk of Deception

Veils of silk that shimmer bright,
Hiding truths from piercing light.
Words like honey, sweet yet sly,
Crafting stories that twist and lie.

Beneath the surface, shadows play,
Trust unraveled, threaded fray.
In this game of dance and chance,
Reality fades in a fleeting glance.

Illusions and Lullabies

Softly sung in twilight's glow,
Melodies of dreams that flow.
Whispers woven in the night,
Cradling hope till morning light.

Illusions flicker, shadows weave,
A tapestry that we believe.
Through lullabies, we drift away,
To lands where worries cease to stay.

Haunting the Corners of Perception

In corners dark where whispers dwell,
Echoes tell a secret spell.
Perceptions shift like grains of sand,
Reality slips from our hands.

Faces shimmering in the haze,
Fading fast, like a fleeting gaze.
Haunted by what we cannot see,
Truth unspools into mystery.

The Charade of Nightfall

In twilight's charm, the shadows creep,
A masquerade where silence weeps.
The stars unveil their secret glow,
While whispered secrets start to flow.

Moonlit faces, veiled in grace,
Dance in the dark, a fleeting trace.
The night hums low, a lover's sigh,
Beneath its cloak, the dreams comply.

Secrets in the Wind

The breezes speak in hushed-toned phrases,
Carrying tales of forgotten mazes.
Leaves rustle softly, secrets shared,
A melody formed from moments bared.

Whispers drift with the autumn air,
Telling of hearts that once laid bare.
Time's gentle hand weaves through the trees,
Easing the burden of memories.

The Silent Watcher

In shadows deep, a presence stays,
The quiet keeper of our days.
With eyes like stars, it softly gleams,
Holding tight to whispered dreams.

It counts the moments, each heartbeat's sound,
In stillness wrapped, where thoughts abound.
A sentinel for hopes and fears,
Cloaked in the fabric of silent years.

Fragments of Forgotten Dreams

In dusty corners, visions fade,
Pieces of hopes in twilight laid.
Splintered memories float in light,
Glimmers of joy from long-lost nights.

Each shard a story, a gentle sigh,
Reflecting the laughter, the reasons why.
Time's gentle hand erodes the seams,
Leaving us fragments of forgotten dreams.

Lurking Between the Lines

In whispers soft, the secrets dwell,
Between the words, they weave their spell.
Each letter holds a trace of night,
Where shadows dance, we seek the light.

A silent breath, a fleeting thought,
In quiet corners, fears are caught.
The pages turn, revealing fate,
Lurking deep, our hearts await.

When lines converge, a story grows,
In hidden paths, the truth bestows.
Yet still we ponder, lost in time,
Each verse a clue, a whispered rhyme.

The margins pulse with unclaimed tales,
In every pause, the silence pales.
Awake the dreams that haunt the night,
Lurking here, just out of sight.

Echoes of Forgotten Dreams

Beneath the stars, the echoes ring,
Of dreams once bright, now lost in spring.
They linger soft like morning dew,
In shadows cast, their whispers grew.

A tender glance, a fleeting sigh,
The past remains as seasons fly.
Each memory, a rustic thread,
In tapestry where spirits tread.

From distant hills, the voices call,
Of wishes, hopes that rise and fall.
In quiet realms, these dreams reside,
Echoes dance where shadows bide.

Yet through the haze, we search for light,
In realms unseen, we take our flight.
To find the paths that once were clear,
In echoes felt, we draw them near.

The Puzzle of Hidden Paths

In tangled woods, the pathways wane,
Where whispers tell of joy and pain.
Each turn a riddle, yet unknown,
The pieces scattered, seeds are sown.

With every step, the forest hums,
A song of fate that never succumbs.
In shadows deep, the answers hide,
The puzzle waits, the heart's true guide.

Between the trees, lost trails reveal,
The space where dreams and fears can heal.
A compass forged in stormy heart,
The hidden paths, a brand new start.

In gentle winds, the secrets sigh,
And beckon forth the soul to try.
To fit the pieces, wild and free,
The puzzle speaks of destiny.

Shadows Playing Tricks

In twilight's glow, the shadows creep,
With mischief wrapped, they come to sweep.
A flicker here, a whisper there,
In games of light, we lose our care.

They stretch and twist, they dance and sway,
Transforming night into the day.
Each corner holds a tale misread,
With shadows weaving dreams instead.

They linger close, so hard to find,
In playful tricks, they bind the mind.
A moment lost, a fleeting blink,
Where truth dissolves in shades of ink.

When dawn breaks through, their essence wanes,
Yet still within, their echo reigns.
For in the dark, we learn to play,
With shadows' tricks that lead astray.

The Dance of Shadows

In the twilight, shadows glide,
Figures flicker, secrets hide.
Whispers twine in soft embrace,
Lost in time, they leave no trace.

Moonlight cast on hidden ground,
Echoes dance without a sound.
Silent stories weave and spin,
In the dark, where dreams begin.

Faintest hints of what was there,
Lingering scents fill the air.
Step in closer, heed the call,
For in shadows, truth may fall.

As the night takes hold of fate,
Shadows twine, they hesitate.
Together in this night so deep,
In their dance, the world will sleep.

Mysterious Currents

Beneath the waves, the secrets flow,
In the depths where no light glows.
Currents twist, they churn and sway,
Guiding thoughts, they drift away.

Whispers of the ocean's song,
Pulling hearts where they belong.
Hidden treasures wait below,
In the dark, their stories grow.

Ripples touch the shores of time,
Echoes pulse in silent rhyme.
Mysterious realms, unseen, unfold,
With every turn, a tale retold.

In the depths, we find our way,
Through the night and to the day.
Let the currents lead us on,
To the wonders just beyond.

The Hidden Map

In the attic, dust and dreams,
A faded map with tangled seams.
X marks places lost in lore,
Secrets waiting at the door.

Lines and curves, a twisting fate,
Key to treasures, love, or hate.
Hidden paths lead far and wide,
With every step, the heart must bide.

Old inscriptions, whispers veiled,
Timeworn tales that once prevailed.
Lost in time, yet found anew,
In the map, life's journey too.

What lies beyond the distant shore?
Adventure waits to be explored.
Follow closely, heed the signs,
For the heart knows where it pines.

Threads of Intrigue

Woven stories, tightly spun,
Secrets shared, but never done.
Whispers linger, tales entwined,
In the labyrinth, truth's confined.

Every thread a path we trace,
Hidden meaning in each space.
Fingers brush the fabric near,
Drawing closer, conquering fear.

Curiosity's gentle pull,
In the heart, a curious lull.
Appearing simple, yet so grand,
The threads bind us, hand in hand.

With each tug, a story brews,
Lives interlaced with vivid hues.
In the tapestry, found we are,
Every thread, a guiding star.

Hidden Patterns of the Night

In the shadows where secrets dwell,
Whispers of dreams begin to swell.
Stars are guides in the darkened skies,
Mapping out tales with silent sighs.

Moonlight weaves through branches bare,
Casting spells on the cool night air.
Each flicker reveals a hidden scheme,
Life's intricate dance, a fleeting dream.

Silhouettes move with quiet grace,
In the mystery of night's embrace.
Patterns flourish in the twilight's gleam,
Creating a world where moments teem.

As dawn approaches, secrets fade,
Yet in the dark, they softly played.
Hidden patterns, forever tight,
Imprinted deep in the fabric of night.

Echoes of the Unseen

In the stillness where thoughts align,
Echoes shimmer, a subtle sign.
Voices carried on the breeze,
Tales of yore wrapped in the trees.

Through the fog, a shadow looms,
Filling spaces, igniting rooms.
Figures dance in the mind's eye,
Leaving whispers as they pass by.

Unseen realms beckon with their song,
Inviting hearts that have gone wrong.
The silence blooms with a soft breath,
A timeless bridge between life and death.

If only we listen closely now,
To the echoes that life avow.
In every silence, a story spins,
Of hidden worlds where truth begins.

The Allure of the Unknown

Beneath the surface, wonders lie,
Chasing shadows, we often sigh.
Curiosity, a guiding flame,
Drawing us forth to play its game.

Paths untraveled call our name,
Whispers promising, never the same.
In the fog, we find our way,
Seeking truths that lead us astray.

Every corner holds a surprise,
Each glance a glimpse of endless skies.
The allure dances, bright yet shy,
A spectrum of dreams that never die.

Hold fast to wonder, let it grow,
In the depths of the unknown flow.
Adventure waits for those who dare,
To chase the mysteries lingering there.

Enigma's Embrace

Wrapped in shadows, secrets play,
The heart yearns for the night’s ballet.
Enigmas breathe in the silence deep,
Where thoughts are tangled, and whispers creep.

Questions linger without reply,
Like clouds drifting in a twilight sky.
Each moment thick with mystery’s trace,
In quiet corners, we seek the grace.

Fingers brush against the unseen,
Unlocking doors where we've never been.
In the dance of fate, shadows collide,
Holding tight to secrets that softly bide.

Embrace the enigma, let it flow,
In every heartbeat, the rhythms grow.
The world unveils its subtle charms,
As we surrender to its open arms.

Shadows of a Stolen Hour

Whispers dance on twilight's breath,
Time slips through like a thief,
Memories linger in the dusk,
Fleeting, yet beyond belief.

Footsteps echo down the lane,
Lost in thought, I chase the dark,
Each shadow holds a secret strain,
With every flicker, a spark.

Stars emerge, their lights awry,
Illuminating paths untold,
In this hour where dreams still lie,
Embraced in silence, bold.

Yet morning calls, the hour fades,
Reality whispers its song,
In the shadows, magic wades,
A stolen hour, where we belong.

In the Heart of a Labyrinth

Twists and turns, where shadows creep,
The walls whisper forgotten lore,
In this maze, the secrets keep,
Searching for an open door.

Each corner hides a tale beneath,
Footprints lead to unseen quests,
In silence, truths unravel, wreath,
Chasing whispers, ghosts as guests.

The heart beats loud, a call so near,
Winding paths both cruel and kind,
In this space, confront your fear,
And lose yourself to find your mind.

With every turn, a choice in hand,
Both stumble and stride in fate's dance,
In the heart of this dreamland,
The labyrinth offers just one chance.

Curious Glances from the Unknown

Beneath the veil of evening's haze,
Eyes emerge from shadows deep,
Curious glances, a wicked gaze,
Secrets through the silence creep.

In the dark, intentions glow,
Like embers in the night's embrace,
Unspoken truths begin to flow,
As whispers weave with every trace.

Time stands still, anticipation,
The world beyond seems far away,
Drawn to this strange attraction,
Where mysteries dance and sway.

With cautious steps, we move as one,
Curiosity ignites the flame,
In the unknown, we've just begun,
A fleeting moment, never the same.

The Jester's Secrets Unfold

In the court where laughter reigns,
A jester twirls with guise and grin,
Behind the mask, dark humor wanes,
Yet secrets whisper deep within.

With every jest, a truth revealed,
A dance of shadows, light refrains,
In playful tones, the heart is healed,
While laughter hides the jester's pains.

Tales of woe wrapped in delight,
The audience lost in the act,
Yet in the jesters' world at night,
Lies a story, cracked but intact.

As the candles flicker low,
And silence grips the raucous crowd,
The jester knows the pain of woe,
In laughter's guise, he stands proud.

Veil of Secrets

Whispers float on the midnight air,
Hidden truths that dare not share.
Wrapped in shadows, a soft embrace,
Eyes like stars, a haunting grace.

In the garden where silence dwells,
Mysteries weave their gentle spells.
Veils of fog conceal the light,
Guarding dreams that take to flight.

A flicker here, a shadow there,
Tales unfold without a care.
In the silence, secrets gleam,
Life is but a fleeting dream.

With every dusk, the veil shall lift,
Revealing truths, a precious gift.
Within the heart, the echoes stay,
Guiding souls along their way.

The Puzzle of Moonlight

Under the glow, the night unravels,
Softly twilight's mystery travels.
Pieces scattered across the night,
Each a clue to find the light.

Reflections dance on silver streams,
Breathing life into our dreams.
The moonlight whispers, calling near,
A puzzle waiting to appear.

Stars align in twinkling rows,
Secrets hidden, only it knows.
With every turn, the shadows play,
Guiding hearts along their way.

In the dark, the light will show,
Paths to follow, seeds to sow.
Together piecing a story bright,
Finding hope in the moon's light.

Shadows Among Us

In the alleys where whispers creep,
Shadows gather, secrets keep.
Figures dance in muted hues,
Foretelling tales the heart can't choose.

Footsteps echo, a haunting sound,
Lost in places where dreams are found.
Among the shadows, spirits play,
Guiding wanderers on their way.

Each corner holds a hidden face,
Woven stories, a timeless grace.
In stillness, they weave and spin,
A tapestry where love begins.

With every twilight, shadows sway,
A gentle reminder they won't stray.
Among us all, they softly tread,
In shared spaces, where dreams are spread.

Riddles in the Dark

In the stillness, riddles lie,
Waiting for a curious sigh.
Questions linger, soft and sweet,
Calling those on restless feet.

The night unfolds its secret page,
Steps of wisdom in every stage.
Through shadows deep, the journey starts,
Leading to the open hearts.

Each riddle holds a piece of light,
Guiding seekers through the night.
With whispered words, the answers sway,
Unraveling the hidden way.

So boldly tread where few have sought,
Embrace the lessons fate has brought.
In the dark, let courage spark,
For every question leaves its mark.

The Labyrinth of the Heart

In the maze of whispers lost,
Each turn a choice, a heavy cost.
With shadows dancing, tales unfold,
A secret love yet to be told.

Through winding paths, I seek the light,
Each heartbeat echoes in the night.
Yearning souls entwined in fate,
The heart's own compass, intricate.

In corners dark, where fears reside,
A flicker glows, a spark inside.
Guiding me with tender grace,
In labyrinths, we find our place.

The journey bends but never ends,
In every twist, the heart transcends.
With every step, a new rebirth,
In the labyrinth of the heart's worth.

Whimsy of the Veiled

Through twilight's hue, the shadows play,
Mysteries wrapped in soft array.
A dance of dreams with whispers light,
The veiled enchantment joins the night.

Laughter echoes, secrets shared,
With fleeting glimpses, souls are bared.
In the chambers where wishes bloom,
The whimsy casts away the gloom.

Beneath the moon's soft, silvery gaze,
A tapestry of forgotten days.
Where every sigh and fleeting glance,
Invites us to a timeless dance.

In playful jest, the spirits tease,
While warming hearts like summer breeze.
In veils of wonder, truth is found,
Whimsy weaves its magic round.

The Spell of Midnight

When darkness falls, the stars ignite,
Whispers wrap the world in night.
A spell is cast, emotions soar,
In midnight's arms, we long for more.

Through hallowed dreams and silent sighs,
The heart unveils its softest cries.
Moonlight drips like honeyed dew,
Enchanting tales of me and you.

As shadows deepen, time stands still,
A magic pulse, electric thrill.
In this sweet hour, secrets tread,
Where words are left, and silence said.

Captive to the night's embrace,
In midnight's weave, we find our place.
A spell woven through every breath,
In twilight's grip, defying death.

Shattered Silhouettes

In fragments bright, our hopes remain,
Scattered pieces bear the pain.
Silent echoes of what was lost,
In shattered dreams, we count the cost.

With every strike, the glass may break,
Yet in the shards, new paths we make.
Reflections dance in twilight's glow,
From brokenness, we learn to grow.

Through haunted halls of love's retreat,
Each silhouette, a heart's heartbeat.
In the chaos, strength will rise,
To mend the cracks beneath the skies.

Embrace the flaws, the tender bends,
In shattered forms, the beauty blends.
We are the light from what once fell,
In unity, we break the spell.

The Mask Behind the Mirror

In shadows cast by flickering light,
A face obscured, within the night.
Reflecting dreams that never show,
The mask I wear, the feelings flow.

Behind the glass, a secret dwells,
Where truth conceals and silence swells.
I search for eyes that feel like home,
Yet find the void, forever roam.

With every glance, the heart unravels,
A journey lost on tangled travels.
Who am I beneath the guise?
A stranger wrapped in whispered lies.

The mirror holds what I can't face,
A longing heart, a fragile place.
To strip away the layers thin,
And find the self I lost within.

Stolen Moments of Wonder

In twilight’s hue, the magic glows,
Where whispered winds and silence flows.
A fleeting glance, a heartbeat's pause,
In stolen moments, life’s a cause.

Beneath the stars, where dreams take flight,
We dance like fireflies in the night.
Each fleeting touch, a secret spun,
In time’s embrace, we become one.

The world stands still, as minutes fade,
In laughter shared, foundations laid.
A captured smile, a breathless chase,
Moments of wonder we embrace.

Life's tapestry, stitched in gold,
In stories shared, our hearts unfold.
With each goodbye, we weave anew,
Stolen moments, forever true.

Secrets in the Mist

Veils of fog, a tender sigh,
Whispers lurking, secrets fly.
Through the haze, shadows creep,
Where memories guide in silence deep.

In dusky trails, the truth hides low,
Faint echoes of what we know.
A lingering thought, a soft embrace,
Within the mist, we find our place.

Figures dance in the shrouded gloom,
As unseen hands brush the room.
With every step, the heartbeats blend,
In the secret where we pretend.

Wrapped in the shroud, we seek and find,
The hidden tales that intertwine.
In the mist, our stories twist,
Lost in secrets that still exist.

Fragments of Eternity

In fleeting moments, time stands still,
Captured breaths, a sacred thrill.
Each smile a piece, a shard of grace,
Fragments of eternity we embrace.

Through passing days, we weave our fate,
In honest hearts, we contemplate.
Every laugh, a timeless key,
Unlocking bonds that set us free.

The world may change, yet love survives,
In every heartbeat, memory thrives.
In whispered hopes, we find our song,
Fragments of time where we belong.

With every tear, the beauty flows,
In patchwork dreams, the spirit glows.
Together we rise, though moments flee,
In fragments of eternity, we're free.

The Unseen Conductor's Symphony

Strings vibrate in a silent night,
Whispers twist in the pale moonlight.
As shadows dance on cool, still ground,
A melody in the air is found.

Notes weave through branches, soft and low,
With every breath, the chorus grows.
The unseen hand guides every sound,
In harmony, the heart is bound.

In dreams where melodies play free,
The echoes speak of what could be.
In concert halls built in the sky,
The music swells, it dares to fly.

A finale whispered on the breeze,
Rides the tide of the rustling leaves.
In twilight's grasp, the symphony sings,
A timeless tale of unseen things.

The Laughter of Hidden Things

In corners where shadows softly cling,
A giggle twirls like a songbird's wing.
In cracks of silence, joy takes flight,
The laughter glows in the pale moonlight.

Beneath the boughs where secrets lie,
Tiny whispers play, a soft sigh.
They dance through the dark, unheard, unseen,
In the magic of night, where we have been.

Fragrant petals release their cheer,
As crickets serenade the ear.
Each twinkling star, a secret shared,
In the garden of dreams, we are ensnared.

With every shadow that plays and prances,
Hidden things invite us to take chances.
Echoes of mirth in the stillness ring,
In the heart of night, the heart takes wing.

Glimmers in the Gloom

In the depths where shadows weave,
Soft sparks of hope gently cleave.
A flicker shines through the dark,
A hidden flame, a secret spark.

Underneath the weight of night,
Whispers flicker, dim yet bright.
They guide the lost on weary trails,
Like tiny ships with wind-filled sails.

Each glimmer tells a tale of old,
Of courage found when the world is cold.
In quiet corners, bright spots grow,
A tapestry of light in woe.

Embrace the flickers, cherish the ray,
In shadows where hope feels far away.
For even in gloom, beauty can bloom,
A path illuminated, banishing doom.

When Candles Flicker and Fade

When candles flicker, shadows blend,
In the twilight, dreams ascend.
Each flame a story, soft and sweet,
A whispered wound of time’s retreat.

Around the edges, darkness sighs,
Echoes of laughter, soft goodbyes.
The waxen tears of moments lost,
In amber glow, we count the cost.

Against the backdrop of silent night,
Flickering thoughts dance in the light.
As shadows wane and spirit grows,
Hope glimmers as the candle glows.

So take this time, let the light guide,
Through fleeting moments, we must abide.
For in the shadows where dreams are laid,
We learn to love, even when they fade.

When the Moon Sings Softly

In the hush of night, she glows,
Casting dreams and soft shadows,
The stars join in a lullaby,
As hearts whisper, and spirits fly.

Crickets chirp their sweet refrain,
Beneath the sky, so vast, so plain,
Each silver beam a gentle kiss,
Painting silence, purest bliss.

The world breathes deep, a calming sigh,
In moonlight's touch, we learn to fly,
With every shimmer, hope ignites,
Glimmers of love in tranquil nights.

So let us dance in silver streams,
Where moonlight weaves our wildest dreams,
Together, lost, yet found in grace,
In the soft embrace of night's warm face.

Unraveled Threads of Fate

In the loom of life, we tread,
Twisting paths where dreams are fed,
Each choice a thread, a pattern spun,
Stories woven, battles won.

But frayed edges tell a tale,
Of winds that blow, of ships that sail,
Through tangled knots and sudden turns,
We find the light, the passion burns.

Fate's gentle hand pulls tight or slack,
Yet onward we walk, we won't look back,
With hearts entwined, we march as one,
Until the course of threads is done.

So gather 'round, let voices blend,
In the mystery that fate can send,
For every thread, though intertwined,
Leads to a fate that’s uniquely designed.

The Game of Silent Whispers

In shadows deep, the secrets lay,
In whispered breaths, they softly sway,
A glance can speak what lips won't dare,
In fleeting moments, truth lays bare.

The echo of a heartbeat's thrum,
Draws wary souls, where silence numbs,
A dance of glances, poised and still,
Fated hearts, igniting will.

Each gesture painted, crafted art,
With every breath, we play our part,
Among the echoes, fears subside,
In the game of whispers, love won't hide.

So let us weave our stories bold,
In the silent spaces, mysteries unfold,
With every secret, every sigh,
The depths of hearts will never lie.

The Riddles of Dusty Corners

In corners dim, where shadows blend,
Whispers linger, stories bend,
Forgotten trinkets, memories cling,
Each dust-filled nook a tale to bring.

The echoes of laughter, time's gentle thief,
Unraveling layers, longing, grief,
Old photographs, a fading smile,
Riddles sleep to beguile a while.

Haunted moments, whispers wise,
Promises made beneath clear skies,
The heart remembers, though time is rust,
Finding meaning in forgotten dust.

So pause and ponder, look within,
For every riddle holds a win,
In dusty corners, truths are spun,
As life whispers softly, our past is won.

The Enchanted Veil

In the forest deep and bright,
A veil of mist, a magical light.
Whispers dance on gentle breeze,
Nature's song among the trees.

Colors blend and shadows sway,
In enchanted moments where dreams play.
Every step, a secret found,
In this realm where hopes abound.

Softly woven, tales unfold,
Stories whispered, truths of old.
Glimmers spark in twilight's glow,
Here in this place where wishes flow.

As night descends, the magic stirs,
The stars align, the heart concurs.
In the enchanted veil we stand,
Together, lost, hand in hand.

Dark Corners of Curiosity

In shadowed realms where whispers creep,
Curiosity wakes from its sleep.
Treading paths of unknown fears,
Seeking truth through hidden tears.

Eyes peer into the void's embrace,
Discovering dreams in a forgotten place.
Questions linger, answers hide,
In dark corners where phantoms bide.

The heart races, the mind ignites,
Dancing with doubt, chasing the nights.
Every secret leads to more,
In the labyrinth where we explore.

Yet through the dark, a spark remains,
Guiding us through the fears and pains.
In curiosity's endless quest,
We find ourselves and learn the rest.

The Mirage of Truth

In the desert vast, the sun beats down,
A shimmering haze creates a frown.
What is real, what is mere sight?
The mirage dances, lost in light.

Footsteps echo on shifting sands,
Chasing illusions with desperate hands.
Each step forward, a twisted fate,
The truth evades; it waits to bait.

The horizon teases, a promise bold,
But every glimpse reveals the cold.
In this endless desert of desire,
We question all, as hopes expire.

Yet through the mirage, we must strive,
To seek the truth, to feel alive.
For in the shimmer lies a clue,
That guides us near to what is true.

Shadows Play Their Game

In twilight's glow, the shadows creep,
They dance with secrets, their secrets to keep.
Laughing softly, they tease the night,
In playful gestures, they take to flight.

Walls echo stories of days gone past,
Where memories wind and shadows cast.
Together they twist, they twirl and sway,
In a world where darkness leads the way.

With every flicker, a story spins,
Of lost loves, of joyful sins.
Their whispers linger like a sweet refrain,
Reminding us gently of love and pain.

So let them play their timeless game,
In every shadow, there's joy, there's shame.
For life itself is but a dance,
In shadows' embrace, we find our chance.

Whispers in the Shadows

In the quiet of the night, shadows play,
Soft whispers drift, where the lost dreams stay.
Moonlight dances on the whispering trees,
Secrets intertwine with the gentle breeze.

Echoes of laughter haunt the lonely streets,
Fading colors blend, where the darkness meets.
Footsteps linger, tracing paths unknown,
In the heart of silence, fears are grown.

Glimmers of hope flicker, yet fade away,
Promises spoken, but in disarray.
The night wraps around like a tender shroud,
Hiding the stories, lost in the crowd.

Beneath the stars, mysteries softly creep,
Awakening visions from the depths of sleep.
In the whispers found, truth and dreams collide,
In the shadows' embrace, we run and hide.

The Enigma's Dance

Underneath the twilight, a figure sways,
A silhouette glimmers in mysterious ways.
With each turn and spin, the secrets unfold,
Tales of yesteryear, in whispers retold.

Her eyes hold the cosmos, vast and deep,
Promises of dreams that never sleep.
With graceful steps, she leads the unknown,
In her enigmatic dance, hearts are sown.

A flicker of laughter, a trace of a tear,
In the rhythm of night, the truth draws near.
Her movements entice, like the moonlit tide,
In the enigma's dance, we dare to confide.

Caught in the moment, we lose our way,
In the song of the night, where shadows play.
With each beat that's played, we follow her trance,
Lost in the magic, the enigma's dance.

Secrets Wrapped in Night

Beneath the stars, the night unfolds,
A tapestry woven with secrets untold.
Whispers of shadows shroud the light,
Embracing the world in the blanket of night.

Figures in silence, moving with grace,
Hidden desires in a forgotten place.
The moon stands witness to the stories we weave,
In the depths of the night, we learn to believe.

Starlit confessions shared with the breeze,
Moments of solace, wrapped like leaves.
Time stands still as the heart takes flight,
In the depths of longing, secrets ignite.

As dawn approaches, the secrets subside,
But memories linger as shadows collide.
For in the night's arms, we dared to ignite,
The warmth of our souls, wrapped in delight.

The Veil of Unseen Faces

In the misty twilight, faces appear,
Softly obscured by the veil of fear.
With stories untold and dreams pressed tight,
They linger in shadows, lost to the light.

Each glance a whisper, each breath a sigh,
Echoes of longing that drift and fly.
Behind the veil, emotions collide,
In the depths of silence, truths cannot hide.

Fingers of mist caress the air,
Brushing the skin, a delicate flare.
The unheard voices beckon us near,
To uncover the stories that fade with the year.

Through the layers of time, they beckon to dance,
Inviting us gently into the trance.
In their mysteries wrapped, we find our place,
In the beauty unseen, within the grace.

Chronicles of the Unexplainable

In whispers soft, the tales unfold,
Of mysteries wrapped in dreams of old.
The night reveals what day conceals,
A dance of fate that time reveals.

With lanterns lit along the way,
We chase the shadows, night and day.
Unraveled threads of fate's design,
In every heart, a secret sign.

The stars above, they softly guide,
Through wretched paths where secrets hide.
A map drawn in the moonlit glow,
An endless quest we dare to know.

In every echo, answers wait,
A puzzle woven through our fate.
With every step, we draw the line,
In chronicles of the divine.

The Secret Languages of the Night

The moonlight whispers soft and clear,
In languages that only we can hear.
The stars confide in twinkling tongues,
A symphony where night is young.

Crickets sing a rhythmic tune,
Beneath the watchful, silver moon.
The rustling leaves share tales of old,
In secrets born from dreams bold.

The world sleeps sound, yet we can see,
The hidden realms where spirits flee.
Each shadow holds a tale untold,
In the dark, our hearts grow bold.

We wander paths of muted light,
Unlocking mysteries of the night.
With every sigh, the stars we trace,
Discovering magic in this space.

Whispers in the Shadows

In quiet corners, secrets breathe,
Soft whispers hide, the heart's reprieve.
Through tangled thoughts and dreams we weave,
In shadows deep, we dare believe.

Each glance exchanged, a story spun,
In twilight's grasp, two souls are one.
The echoes linger, soft and low,
In hushed tones, the truths we know.

The night enfolds us, warm embrace,
A dance of time, a fleeting trace.
In gentle currents, hearts align,
While shadows hold what feels divine.

With every breath, the world we change,
In whispered vows, no love is strange.
Together lost, together found,
In shadows' depth, our dreams resound.

Enigmatic Echoes

Across the void, the echoes call,
Of mysteries that bind us all.
In fleeting moments, glances meet,
In resonating heartbeats, sweet.

The past, a ghost that lingers near,
With every sigh, we draw it here.
Each story told, a spark ignites,
Revealing truths in starry nights.

We trace the lines of fate's design,
In every whisper, wisdom shines.
The shadows dance to music sweet,
In echoes low, our souls entreat.

Through labyrinths of time and space,
We find ourselves in love's embrace.
In every heartbeat, every sigh,
Enigmatic echoes never die.

The Dance of Illusions

In shadows cast by flickering light,
Figures sway in the hush of night.
Dreams entwine with whispered sighs,
As illusion dances, truth often lies.

A twirl of colors, a fleeting glance,
Caught in the web of a mystic trance.
Reality bends, a fragile frame,
Lost in the heartbeat of a phantom flame.

Masks parade in a masquerade ball,
Each step a riddle, tempting us all.
Through veils of smoke, we chase the sound,
In the dance of illusions, we're forever bound.

With each pirouette, we fall and rise,
Chasing the echoes of shifting skies.
In this theater of dreams, we play our parts,
Dancing on strings of forgotten hearts.

Curious Haze

In the morning light, a fog descends,
Blurring the lines where the journey ends.
Whispers linger in the cool, crisp air,
As mysteries beckon with a gentle stare.

Footsteps wander on a winding street,
Each corner turned, a secret to greet.
In the labyrinth of thoughts, I lose my way,
Chasing the dreams that dare to sway.

Faded memories intertwine with today,
In the curious haze, they flicker and play.
Voices echo in a melodic dance,
Inviting souls to take a chance.

Through the veil of mist, a truth may gleam,
In the curious haze, we awaken the dream.
With every breath, a new tale unfolds,
In the heart of the haze, our story is told.

Secrets Wrapped in Silence

In the quiet corners where shadows lie,
Secrets linger without a sigh.
Whispers drift on the cool night air,
Wrapped in silence, they linger there.

Words unspoken, a hidden trust,
In the depths of silence, secrets rust.
Eyes that shimmer with untold tales,
In the stillness, the heart unveils.

Moments captured in a soft embrace,
Silent vows in a sacred space.
Each heartbeat echoes a gentle plea,
For the truth that waits, yet dares to be free.

In this haven of secrets, we find our way,
Wrapped in silence, come what may.
Through the layers of stillness, we learn to see,
The beauty that lies in what cannot be.

Echoes of Forbidden Paths

Through the thorns where shadows creep,
Echoes whisper in secrets deep.
A forbidden path, elusive and dark,
Leading the brave to a lost spark.

Footsteps falter, yet hearts ignite,
Chasing dreams that flee from sight.
In every turn, a haunting sound,
Echoes of souls that once were found.

Moonlight dances on an ancient stone,
Where silence reigns and spirits roam.
Through tangled roots and distant calls,
The path beckons as the night falls.

To wander these trails is to seek the truth,
In echoes of laughter, the innocence of youth.
Though forbidden, the journey unfolds,
In the heart of the night, adventure unfolds.

The Riddle of the Stars

In the night, they dance and twirl,
Whispering secrets to the world.
Planets spin in endless grace,
While visions of dreams interlace.

A constellation's tale unfolds,
Mysteries in stardust told.
Each flicker tells a story,
Of hope and ancient glory.

Beneath the moon's soft embrace,
We ponder time and space.
Galaxies in silent flight,
Guide us through the darkest night.

In the void, we seek to find,
The riddles left behind.
A journey through the cosmic sea,
To uncover what we’re meant to be.

Echoes of Betrayal

In shadows deep, trust laid bare,
Whispers linger in the air.
The heart, once whole, now fractured,
By promises that love has captured.

Every glance, a dagger's kiss,
A longing for the moments missed.
With each word, a silent scream,
As hope dissolves like a fleeting dream.

Ghosts of love haunt every space,
Familiar paths, now filled with grace.
Yet in the echoes, pain remains,
A melody of heart's refrains.

We weave through lies, fragile threads,
Bearing burdens in our heads.
Yet somehow, we find a way,
To heal from echoes of betrayal.

The Alluring Abyss

Gaze into the swirling deep,
Where shadows and secrets seep.
A world beneath the glimmering tide,
Invites the brave to take a ride.

With sirens' call, the depths entice,
Mysteries wrapped in restless ice.
The lure of darkness, rich and rare,
Pulls at the heart, beyond despair.

In the silence, whispers float,
As dreams and fears begin to gloat.
The abyss sings a haunting tune,
Creating echoes beneath the moon.

Yet in that darkness, light may bloom,
Hope can rise from depths of gloom.
In the abyss, we learn to see,
The beauty of our own decree.

Captivating Uncertainties

In a world where paths entwine,
Questions linger, dimly shine.
Every step, a dance unplanned,
With fate's brush upon our hand.

The future whispers, soft and sly,
While dreams flicker, laugh, and fly.
With each choice, a fork appears,
Leading us through laughter and tears.

Shifting winds of chance embrace,
Every moment, a new face.
To trust the journey, wander free,
Is to find our destiny.

In uncertainties, we find gold,
Stories waiting to be told.
With open hearts, we shall explore,
The captivating forevermore.

Gentle Taps on the Windowpane

A whisper of rain begins to fall,
Gentle taps echo, nature's call.
Soft drumming on glass, a soothing sound,
In quiet moments, peace is found.

The world outside, a muted gray,
Carried dreams of a brighter day.
Each droplet tells a fleeting tale,
As memories drift like a soft-gone sail.

The dance of light, in shadows play,
Caressing thoughts, as night turns day.
Emotions rise with each tender beat,
In harmony, our hearts repeat.

As evening falls, the storm subsides,
With every tap, a melody rides.
The windowpane, a canvas bare,
Reflects the love we choose to share.

Labyrinthine Secrets Linger

In twisted halls where shadows creep,
Ancient secrets quietly sleep.
Whispers echo through the maze,
Inviting souls to wander and gaze.

Corners turned with bated breath,
Each path a choice, a dance with death.
A flicker of light breaks the gloom,
Hope emerges, dispelling doom.

The heart beats fast in this test of fate,
Finding courage in each twist of weight.
Unraveling knots of lies and truth,
Revealing wisdom lost in youth.

In every turn, a lesson learned,
Within the labyrinth, our spirits burned.
Secrets linger, waiting to bide,
For those brave enough to step inside.

Tangles of Time and Space

Threads of moments, woven tight,
In the fabric of day and night.
Time flows gently, a river vast,
Moments stretch, but never last.

Echoes linger in the air,
Memories find us unaware.
With each tick, the world spins on,
In tangled knots, our fears are drawn.

Waves of time crash on the shore,
Whispers of what came before.
Fleeting glances of yesteryear,
Light the path that we hold dear.

Space entwines with every breath,
In this dance, we hold no death.
Tangles weave, creating grace,
In every heartbeat, we find our place.

Surprises Beneath the Surface

Beneath the stillness lies the deep,
Where secrets stir, and shadows creep.
Ripples fade but stories grow,
In hidden depths, the truths will flow.

A flicker glimmers past the veil,
Mysteries wrapped in a gentle trail.
What seems calm can twist and sway,
Revealing wonders on display.

Time holds treasures, carefully laid,
In silence, hopes and dreams are weighed.
Dive beneath, embrace the unknown,
For in the depths, true gems are shown.

Surprises await those brave enough,
To seek adventure, to get tough.
With every stir, the heart can soar,
For beneath the surface, there's always more.

Veiled Intentions

In whispered tones, the shadows weave,
A tapestry where hearts believe.
Behind the veil, a story lies,
Of dreams deferred and silent sighs.

Eyes darting quick, intent concealed,
A fragile truth, forever healed.
Beneath the surface, currents flow,
In veiled intentions we seldom show.

Promises etched in shadows deep,
Secrets shared, yet none will keep.
With every glance, a silent plea,
In hidden thoughts, we long to be.

Yet hope ignites, a fire bright,
Through dotted paths of day and night.
Perhaps one day, we'll lift the shroud,
And speak our truths, resolute and loud.

The Lure of Shadows

In twilight's grasp, where secrets play,
The lure of shadows draws us away.
Beneath the moon's soft, silver gaze,
We dance with whispers, lost in a haze.

Figures flicker, silhouettes stand,
In the embrace of night, we hand in hand.
What lies beyond the boundary thin?
A world awakened, where dreams begin.

A longing spark ignites the soul,
In shadow's arms, we feel most whole.
With every step, a heartbeat thumps,
To rhythms known in quiet hums.

So take my hand, let's drift away,
Into the dusk, where shadows sway.
Together we'll explore the night,
Until the dawn brings back the light.

Masks of the Unrevealed

In crowded rooms, we play our part,
Wearing masks that hide the heart.
A smile painted, laughter's guise,
But deeper truths evade the eyes.

Each mask a shield from life's cruel art,
Yet underneath, we feel the start.
Fingers trembling, yearning to break,
To shed the skin and dare to wake.

The world spins on, with faces bright,
Concealing shadows, dimming light.
But in still moments, truths appear,
Unveiling depths we long to clear.

Let’s lay aside the worn disguise,
And greet the dawn with open eyes.
For in the light, we find our way,
To love the masks and stay the day.

Hushed Secrets in the Breeze

The summer air holds secrets soft,
In whispers that the wind lifts aloft.
With leaves that rustle tales untold,
And memories wrapped in threads of gold.

As twilight deepens, shadows blend,
Nature hums of love and mend.
Each breath a promise, every sigh,
In the hush of dusk, we learn to fly.

With every gust, a story's spun,
Of laughter shared and battles won.
Under starlit skies, we roam,
In the breeze, we feel at home.

So let the breeze carry our dreams,
Where hope ignites in gentle beams.
For in the hush of winds that tease,
We find our truth in whispered breeze.

Echoes of the Unexplored

Whispers in the ancient trees,
Calling out to those who seek.
Footsteps on a path unmade,
Echoes of the dreams we keep.

Flickers of a hidden light,
Guide the wanderers who roam.
In the silence, truths take flight,
Mapping out a brand new home.

Every shadow holds a tale,
Every breeze a secret song.
In this world, we dare to sail,
In the dark, where we belong.

Voices rise from distant shores,
Tales of lands yet to be known.
In the heart, adventure roars,
In the wild, we're not alone.

The Enigma Unfolds

Glimmers in the twilight haze,
Mysteries await their chance.
Flickering like candle flames,
In the night, we start to dance.

Curiosity ignites,
Questions linger on our lips.
With each heartbeat, truth ignites,
As we delve into eclipse.

Step by step, the puzzle grows,
Piece by piece, we find our way.
In the silence, knowledge flows,
Guiding dreams that dare to play.

Every turn a chance to learn,
Every thought a seed to sow.
In the dark, our passions burn,
As the enigma starts to glow.

Secrets Beneath the Surface

Ripples dance on waters deep,
Hiding truths beneath the waves.
Silent whispers we must keep,
In the dark, the past behaves.

Beneath the calm, the storms do rise,
Each crest a story left untold.
Within the depths, we seek the prize,
Unlocking secrets, brave and bold.

Every shadow tells a tale,
Of dreams that long to see the light.
In this dance, we shall prevail,
Turning darkness into bright.

From the depths we draw our breath,
Embracing all that lies below.
In the journey, there is death,
Yet life anew begins to grow.

Underneath the Surface

Layers deep, our stories lie,
Hidden truths beneath the skin.
In the stillness, we can cry,
Underneath where dreams begin.

Veins of gold and heart of stone,
Life's a tapestry we weave.
Every thread a life we own,
In the fabric, we believe.

Quiet moments spark with light,
Glimmers of what we could be.
In the shadows, hope takes flight,
Healing as it sets us free.

Underneath the noise and fuss,
Lies the core of who we are.
In the silence, wait for us,
For we shine just like a star.

Ensnared by Enigmas

In shadows deep, the whispers play,
Where riddles dance and secrets stay.
A puzzle formed in darkened skies,
Each clue a mask, a thin disguise.

Chasing hints through twisted lanes,
We seek the truth that ever wanes.
Each turn a trap, each path a test,
To unveil mysteries, we feel oppressed.

Yet in the twilight, hope ignites,
A spark of light among the bites.
With heart as compass, we pursue,
The tangled web that leads to you.

Together we will find our way,
Through every shade of gray we sway.
For in each enigma's grasp we find,
The strength of souls forever twined.

Under the Fog of Night

Beneath the veil where silence lingers,
The night reveals her ghostly fingers.
Stars are hidden, dreams unfold,
In whispers soft and stories told.

The moon a sentinel, watches high,
While shadows weave, and creatures sigh.
A world unknown, where spirits roam,
In every heart, a longing home.

Through misty pathways, we explore,
Each step a chance to seek and soar.
For in the darkness, wonders gleam,
Illuminating every dream.

As dawn approaches, shadows wane,
The secrets spoken, joys remain.
Under the fog, our journeys start,
The night embraced within our heart.

The Traces of Solitude

In quiet corners, echoes dwell,
Each footstep soft, a tale to tell.
Whispers of thoughts that drift away,
In solitude's arms, we silently stay.

The moments stretch like shadows lost,
Counting the beats, we bear the cost.
Layers of silence, comfort and fright,
In every heartbeat, soul takes flight.

With ink-stained pages, memories write,
Emotions woven like stars at night.
Through woven threads, we softly trace,
The quiet landscape of empty space.

In solitude’s grasp, we learn to see,
The beauty found in just being free.
For in the stillness, we can unfold,
The deepest joys that silence holds.

Clues Beneath the Surface

Beneath the waters, secrets hide,
In currents swift, where dreams collide.
The surface stirs, but underneath,
Lie stories waiting, void of breath.

With gentle ripples, we dive in deep,
To uncover treasures, secrets keep.
Each bubble rising, holds a tale,
A whispering voice, a ghostly wail.

In depths unseen, perception shifts,
Invisible lines where truth now drifts.
The weight of silence, stories unfold,
In every shadow, a fragment of gold.

We chart the course of what we find,
With every clue, we redefine.
Beneath the surface, the world ignites,
Revealing wonders hidden from sight.

The Clandestine Dance

Underneath the silver moon,
Figures glide in shadowed gloom.
Whispers echo through the night,
Where secrets twist in soft moonlight.

In hidden glades, they spin and sway,
Each movement whispers, 'Come and play.'
The night air shimmers with desire,
Their hearts ablaze, a silent fire.

Caught between the worlds they tread,
In dreams and darkness, lightly wed.
With every turn, the stars align,
In this sacred space, divine.

As dawn begins to break the spell,
They vanish with a silent yell.
Yet in the day, their whispers stay,
In the heart's chambers, they will play.

Chasing Phantom Footprints

Along the shore, I walk alone,
Chasing echoes, softly grown.
Footprints left by those unseen,
Ghostly paths where I have been.

The tide erases every trace,
Yet still I feel that phantom grace.
Each step I take, a fleeting glance,
Into the depths of time's strange dance.

In the moonlight, shadows blend,
To past and future, I descend.
They lead me on, a mystic trail,
Through whispers soft, I must not fail.

And as the sun begins to rise,
I chase the dreams that cloak the skies.
For every step, a story speaks,
In fleeting moments, love still seeks.

Secrets Beneath the Surface

The river flows, a silken thread,
Where dreams and wishes often bled.
Beneath its calm, the truth may hide,
In depths where shadows twist and glide.

With each soft ripple, tales unfold,
Of daring hearts and spirits bold.
The currents whisper, secrets raw,
In gentle waves, the world in awe.

Mysterious depths of dark and light,
Hold ancient sorrows out of sight.
Yet those who dare to dive so deep,
May find the truths the surface keeps.

So listen close, the water sings,
Of hidden gems and broken wings.
In every drop, a story waits,
To be unveiled before it fades.

The Labyrinth of Whispers

In a maze where shadows play,
Whispers guide me on my way.
Each turn reveals a hidden truth,
The essence lost, the voice of youth.

Walls of ivy seep with lore,
As echoes linger, wanting more.
I wander deeper into night,
With every breath, my fears take flight.

The silence speaks, it calls my name,
Intangible yet wild and tame.
In corridors of dreams I roam,
Seeking solace, searching home.

But as I tread this winding track,
I find my heart will not look back.
For in this maze, I've come to see,
The labyrinth holds the key to me.

Veiled Intentions at Dusk

Shadows gather on the ground,
Secrets whispered, barely found.
As night falls, intentions hide,
Underneath the twilight's tide.

Fleeting moments, time does bend,
What is truth, and where's the end?
Masked in dusk, the hearts align,
Veiled intentions intertwine.

Eyes that glimmer, thoughts concealed,
Stories woven, yet revealed.
In the silence, tensions grow,
What lies beneath? We may not know.

As the stars begin to gleam,
Reflecting shadows, like a dream.
Here we dance, in twilight's blush,
Embracing all, in evening's hush.

The Mischief of Wandering Thoughts

Thoughts like leaves, they sway and dart,
Chasing echoes, they depart.
A whisper here, a memory there,
Fleeting fancies, light as air.

In the stillness, they conspire,
Fueling dreams, igniting fire.
What is real? What slips away?
In this chase, we often stray.

A stolen glance, a fleeting smile,
Moments cherished for a while.
Wandering thoughts, a playful jest,
Carrying our hearts, unguessed.

Through the maze of shadows cast,
Embrace the present, hold it fast.
In the chaos, find your peace,
Let the wandering thoughts release.

Jests of the Midnight Breeze

A soft caress, the night awakes,
Whispers play with silver lakes.
The wind, a thief of silent dreams,
Stealing thoughts in moonlit beams.

It dances lightly through the trees,
Bringing jests from far-off seas.
With playful tricks, it pulls our hair,
A subtle tease, a gentle dare.

Echoes linger in the dark,
Flickering like a distant spark.
The midnight breeze, a fleeting thief,
Bringing joy, or offering grief.

Underneath the starry dome,
It carries laughter, it feels like home.
Jests of night, so wild and bold,
Their stories often left untold.

The Cloak of Uncertainty

Wrapped in shadows, doubts arise,
Veiled in mist, truth often lies.
A path unknown, yet we must tread,
In this cloak, we forge ahead.

Questions flutter like the leaves,
In the wind, what fate deceives?
With every step, we question still,
What’s our heart’s enduring will?

Moments linger, heavy air,
In uncertainty, we lay bare.
Yet in the fog, a spark ignites,
Guiding souls through restless nights.

Embrace the shroud, the fears that breed,
For in the darkness, there’s a seed.
From doubt's embrace, we find our way,
As dawn breaks forth to light the day.

Tides of Intrigue

Whispers dance upon the shore,
Secrets hidden, tales of lore.
Currents pull, both fierce and sly,
Eyes of shadows, watch them fly.

In the depths, a siren's call,
Echoes through the silent hall.
Moonlight glimmers on the crest,
Hearts entwined in fleeting jest.

From the depths, desires swell,
Broken dreams, a silent knell.
Tales of longing, drawn anew,
Caught between the old and true.

Waves recede as truths dissolve,
Mysteries we can't resolve.
Yet the tides will bring again,
Whispers lost in heart's refrain.

The Silent Jest

In shadows deep, they gather round,
Echoing laughter, not a sound.
Eyes alight with secret glee,
Hidden truths, a mystery.

A jest is cast in whispered tones,
Beneath the guise of ancient stones.
Wit entwined with fate's design,
In every pause, the stars align.

Behind the mask, a playful grin,
Life's illusion wears so thin.
The silent jest, the knowing grin,
A game of chance where hearts begin.

In quiet halls where shadows play,
We weave our fates, both night and day.
Amidst the laughter, truths emerge,
In silent jest, our spirits surge.

Cloaked in Twilight

As day surrenders to the night,
The world is cloaked in dusky light.
Shadows stretch and softly blend,
A whispered promise, dusk will mend.

The stars awaken, one by one,
Guiding souls till night is done.
In twilight's grasp, a dance unfolds,
Secrets spun, in dreams retold.

Ancient trees in silent sighs,
Murmur tales beneath the skies.
In this hush, the heart can breathe,
Cloaked in twilight, we believe.

Time may fade, yet we remain,
Bound by dusk, in joy or pain.
With every twilight, love ignites,
In the shadows, pure delight.

Unraveled Threads of Fate

In the loom where moments weave,
Strands of life, which we perceive.
With every tug, a story frays,
Unraveled threads in fleeting days.

Destinies twist like strands of gold,
Secrets held, yet to unfold.
In the tapestry of time,
Whispers echo, lost in rhyme.

Fate's design can alter fast,
Shadows linger of the past.
Each knot a choice, each fray a chance,
In the dance of life's expanse.

As we weave, let hearts entwine,
In the patterns, love will shine.
Through the chaos, we'll create,
A masterpiece, unraveled fate.

The Allure of Shadows

In twilight's grasp, whispers reign,
Shadows dance, a silken chain.
They weave through trees, a secret flight,
Embracing dreams that fade from sight.

Beneath the moon, they softly creep,
Guarding tales that silence keep.
In every corner, dark they loom,
Yet in their depths, a hidden bloom.

A flicker here, a silhouette there,
Teasing minds, a silent dare.
To chase the dark, to seek the light,
In shadows' play, we find our plight.

Their allure calls, a bit of night,
A fleeting glimpse, a shiver of fright.
Yet through this dance, the heart may find,
A deeper truth, entwined, aligned.

Vanishing Trails

Paths once trodden, fade from view,
Memory's echo, a gentle cue.
Footsteps lost in the morning dew,
Whispers of journeys, brave and true.

Winding ways lead to the unknown,
Each turn reveals what seeds have grown.
Yet in the brush, the past remains,
A fading song that still retains.

Underneath the boughs, a trace,
Of those who've wandered, left their place.
Each step a story, now untold,
Vanishing trails, both warm and cold.

Yet as we seek, new paths will form,
In the heart's journey, a quiet storm.
To vanish is not to be erased,
For every trail, a life embraced.

The Enigmatic Path

A winding road through mist and trees,
Holds secrets whispered on the breeze.
Curled in shadows, tales unfold,
Each step a mystery to behold.

Footprints lead where few have trod,
An adventure whispered by the God.
Each twist and turn, a choice to make,
In the enigmatic, hearts awake.

Through light and dark, the path does weave,
Inviting souls who dare believe.
With every turn, the unknown glows,
And in the journey, wisdom grows.

So venture forth, embrace the strange,
For in the unknown, life can change.
With open hearts, we seek the light,
On the enigmatic path, take flight.

Curious Whispers

In corners dim, where shadows dwell,
Curious whispers weave their spell.
They drift like smoke, elusive, free,
Sharing secrets, a silent plea.

Amidst the night, they softly sigh,
Carrying tales, as time floats by.
Every voice, a phantom dream,
Echoing hopes, a gentle seam.

With eyes closed tight, we lean to hear,
The whispered truths that draw us near.
In every echo, a story spins,
Of all that losses and all that wins.

So listen close, let silence guide,
In curious whispers, hearts confide.
For in each note, a bond we find,
In whispered truths, our souls entwined.